MW00906006

The MANY CARTOON FACES of
DANNY!

Kevin Tobin

St. John's, Newfoundland and Labrador
2010

Canada Council for the Arts   Conseil des Arts du Canada

Canadä

We gratefully acknowledge the financial support of the Canada Council for the Arts, the Government of Canada through the Book Publishing Industry Development Program (BPIDP), and the Government of Newfoundland and Labrador through the Department of Tourism, Culture and Recreation for our publishing program.

Illustrations © 2010, Kevin Tobin
Cover design © 2010, Derek Mills
Layout by Todd Manning

Published by
CREATIVE PUBLISHERS
an imprint of CREATIVE BOOK PUBLISHING
a Transcontinental Inc. associated company
P.O. Box 8660, St. John's,
Newfoundland and Labrador
A1B 3T7

Printed in Canada by:
Transcontinental Inc.

Printed on acid-free paper

First Printing October 2010
Second Printing December 2010

Library and Archives Canada Cataloguing in Publication

Tobin, Kevin, 1958-
Danny : the many cartoon faces of / Kevin Tobin.

Cartoons.
ISBN 978-1-897174-64-7

1. Williams, Danny, 1949- –Caricatures and cartoons. 2. Premiers (Canada)–Newfoundland and Labrador–Caricatures and cartoons. 3. Newfoundland and Labrador–Politics and government–21st century–Caricatures and cartoons. 4. Canadian wit and humor, Pictorial. I. Title.

NC1449.T61A4 2010   971.8'050207   C2010-904961-6

To Joey, Frank, Brian, Tom, Clyde, Brian, Beaton, Roger and Danny. I love you guys.

INTRODUCTION

In 2002, as Brian Tobin (no relation) was winding down his once-promising days as the sixth premier of our province, I was also starting to lose a step or two in the editorial cartooning biz. Newfoundland and Labrador politics has always been dominated by a couple of colourful characters. And that usually made my job a little easier and a lotta fun. Always an issue...always a controversial figure...just figure out what I wanted to say...and draw it. More or less.

Tobin hit the scene federally during the Great Crosbie era – and between them and Clyde, I was kept pretty busy cartooning for The Telegram for a decade or so...always something to fire me up.

With Tobin now gone, I was burnt out. The subsequent premiers afterwards caused a little commotion for me to draw upon...but no real passion or spark. Truly, I was thinking that maybe, I too, should join my namesake and step aside. Maybe I had nothing left to say...or draw.

Enter a new, fresh Mullet in provincial politics. Enter Danny Williams.

First, as Leader of the Official Opposition. Then, in 2003, elected as Premier of Newfoundland and Labrador. Colourful and controversial, Danny represented many things to the many voters – a fighter; a lawyer; a millionaire businessman; oil baron; dictator to some; and finally, the Popular Supreme Leader and Glorious Spiritual Guide!

And for me, he became the Viagra I needed to fire up the old creative juices again. Thanks, Danny.

I first "met" Danny Williams about five years ago at Mile One Centre in St. John's. I was watching a hockey game with my son Shane, when I could see the premier mixing with the crowd and bleacher creatures in the stands. Now I should say that ever since Shane realized that I drew cartoons and kinda poked fun at some people, he was very concerned and protective of me. Even at his very young age at the time, he imagined that some politician might be offended by my cartoon of them...and even approach me to give me a piece of their mind. Or piece of two by four!

Seeing Danny and his "bodyguards" in the stands gave me an idea. As in most of my cartoons, inspiration hit me fast. I chuckled to myself as I was about to play a little trick on my son.

"Look, Shane, there's Danny Williams, the Premier...in the stands...up there," I yelled to my son. Then I quickly jumped to my feet and waved my arms crazily like someone wanting to be rescued from a deserted island by a passing ship...and started screaming and roaring my head off..."DANNY! DANNY! OVER HERE! OVER HERE!" Shane was horrified! He couldn't believe it. He thought Danny was going to come down and tackle me. Or have me dragged out of the arena by his angry mob and thrown in jail. "DANNY, DANNY," I kept yelling, "It's me. IT'S ME!"

After a second or two of thinking all hell was going to break out, Shane jumped up on his seat and tried to block my view of Danny...or his view of me. In this big, loud stadium, I knew Danny couldn't hear or see me, but Shane didn't know that.

After I burst out laughing at his reaction, Shane cautiously realized it was just a little joke. But, not knowing when to say when, I kept jumping up and trying to get Danny's attention a few more times that evening. And Shane still reluctantly tried to block me and quiet me down. He kept one eye on me and one on Danny to make sure we weren't both going to cause another scene. Thanks, Shane.

Later, that evening, I actually briefly introduced myself to Danny outside the men's washroom. It was very civilized and gentlemanly-like. Nobody got dragged off to the Pen. Secretly, I really wanted to develop a scheme between us where he would actually approach Shane and me in the stands and pretend to be extremely angry with me and my cartoons of him. I didn't ask...but it could have been lots of fun. Right, Shane?

Of course, it never happened. It's weird, though...but in a way, I feel that Danny and I are kinda like a duo. He creates the buzz...I draw him buzzing around. We're a team, in a way. Sonny and Cher. Peckford and Sprung. Good cop... bad cop.

Even heroes need villains.

FOREWORD

BY FABIAN MANNING

I believe there exists a passion in the politics of Newfoundland and Labrador that is unequalled and difficult to explain with just the written word. For many years, Kevin Tobin, through his editorial cartoons has given a colour to the political landscape of our Province that mere words could never express. While Kevin's work continues to address issues of a serious nature they do so with an ever enjoyable dash of humour, and we are all aware that humour is part of our heritage and the core of our culture. It is one of the main reasons we have been able to survive on this rock in the Atlantic Ocean for over 500 years.

This collection of Kevin's work depicts the political life of our current Premier Danny Williams. Since assuming the Premier's office in October 2003, Danny has been and continues to be a powerful political force here at home and abroad. Whatever your opinion of the man, I believe we all would agree that he has changed how we look at ourselves and maybe more importantly, how others now look at us.

Throughout the pages of this book you will be reminded of some of the highlights of Danny's tenure as our Premier. From the early battles with Leo Puddister and NAPE, from Prime Minister Stephen Harper to the Days of ABC, from Eastern Health to Hydro Quebec – Kevin has captured all of it in what I like to refer to as "Tobin's Masterpiece of Miniature".

There are many different sides to 'Our Danny' and I have witnessed a few of those myself. Whether it was sitting around enjoying a joke or story and sharing a laugh in 'The Early Days' or experiencing his Irish Blood Boil, I truly believe that the good Lord threw away the mould when he created Danny.

Looking at things in the positive light from my experience with Danny I can attest to the fact that there is a side of him that has a tremendous sense of humour. I believe he will enjoy this collection of Kevin's work and my wish is that you do also.

God Bless!!

DANNY MILLIONS

RESERVED
PREMIER
the Telegram
KT
2003.

I'M THE HIPHOP MAN
FOR NEWFOUNDLAND...
I'LL RANT 'N' ROAR
FOR LABRADOR...
BUSTA GRIMES
GOT NO MORE
RHYMES...
IT'S TIME —
FOR PUFF DANNY
TO TAKE THE FLOOR!
NY
2003.

OIL
DANNY
DUBYA...
2004
KT

NO, CANADA!
NO, CANADA! OUR HOME IS NEWFOUNDLAND!
WE WON'T FLY THE FLAG WHILE MARTIN'S IN COMMAND...
WITH BROKEN HEARTS, THERE'LL BE NO MORE TALKS,
'TIL WE GET OUR OIL MON-EY!
IT WAS DO OR DIE, NO CANADA,
WE WON'T BACK DOWN FROM THEE.
YOUR UNFAIR DEMANDS WON'T BRING US TO OUR KNEES
NO, CANADA, WE'LL KEEP OUR DIGNITY,
NO, CANADA, WE'LL KEEP OUR DIGNITY!
KT 2004.
The Telegram

SOMEWHERE IN BARBADOS, DANNY IS ENJOYING A WELL-DESERVED BREAK...
I SAID THE GOVERNMENT DOESN'T HAVE ANY MONEY... —NOT ME!
ONE WAY TO BEAT THE FREEZE!
2004.
KT
the Telegram.

DANNY'S COSTUME FOR HALLOWEEN...
I DON'T VANT A CAP–I VANT TO COUNT! ONE MILLION... TWO MILLION...
AH... AH... AH...
2004.
The Telegram
Happy Halloween BOO

DANNY
TRUMP
YOU'RE FIRED!
2004.
KT.

SWINGIN' HIGH ABOVE THE CONFEDERATION BUILDING,
IT'S SPIDER DAN...
MENACE OR HERO?
2004
KT.

2005
KT.
The Telegram
OH! THIS IS THE PLACE WHERE
THE MILLIONAIRES GATHER...
WITH OIL FIELDS AND GBS DRILLS BORIN' DOWN.
ALL SIZES OF RIGGERS MAKE OUR
POCKETS GROW BIGGERS...
LET'S CELEBRATE HERE
ON THE
OIL RIGGIN' GROUND!
DANNY PLANKERIN'
DOWN WITH HIS ATLANTIC
ACCORDION...

2005.
STAND BY YOUR DAN...
MARTIN SINGING THE PRAISES OF OUR DANNY BILLIONS...

EXCELLENT, LOYOLA...
DANNY 'BURNS'
ANOTHER SENIOR CIVIL SERVANT...
the Telegram 2005
KT

NEWFOUNDLAND AND LABRADOR
HYDRO'S NEW MASCOT—
"DANNY'S READY
KILOWATT"...
2006
The Telegram

WHAT'S WRONG WITH FPI
FISH PLANT WORKERS
TAKING A ROLLBACK?
I GO TO THE BANK EVERYDAY
AND TAKE A ROLL BACK!
$1000
2006

OBI-DAN KENOBI
SHORE WARS
HUM
HUM
HUM
HUM
HUM
JOIN NEWFOUNDLAND'S JEDI MASTER IN HIS CONTINUING BATTLE WITH OTTAWA ON OFFSHORE OIL & GAS AND EQUALIZATION...
KT
2006

ALL I'M TRYING TO DO IS MAKE SURE EVERYONE HAS MORE FIBRE IN THEIR DIET...
NEW
FIBRE
OPTIC
CEREAL
KENMORE
PERSONA
ROGERS
MTS ALLSTREAM
The Telegram 2006
KT

ROGERS "OUT of the FOG" presents
DANcing with the Star!
...YOU CAN DO THE TORY TANGO, THE HARPER HUSTLE OR THE OFFSHORE CHA CHA WITH DAN THE DANCING SENSATION!
YOUR PHOTO HERE.
2006.
KT

...5 PLUS GOLDEN RINGS (FOR MHAs)...
$4.4 MILLION (SCANDAL)...
3 PARTIES INVOLVED...
2 MUCH OVERSPENDING...
AND A FRAZZLED PREMIER VACATIONING IN THE PALM TREES!
KT 2006
The Telegram

NOIA?! MORE LIKE YESIA!!!
THIS TIME, DANNY BRINGS HOPE (AND A DIFFERENT FINGER) TO OIL AND GAS CONFERENCE...
2007.
KT

"ANYONE WHO MAKES US POLITICIANS LOOK BAD IN THE EYES OF THE PUBLIC SHOULD BE SUED — WHAT ARE YOU LOOKIN' AT?"

MR. PREMIER, SIR... ARRIVING FOR THE FALL SITTING OF THE HOUSE OF ASSEMBLY...
KEEP 'ER RUNNIN', JAMES— I WON'T BE LONG...
2008.
KT
The Telegram

UNIONS,
TAKE IT OR
TAKE YOUR
CHANCES...
TWENTY PERCENT
WAGE OFFER
OIL
OVER A BARREL...?

Ha-Ha!
UNIONS

KT.
2009
IF I HAD 800 MILLION DOLLARS
I'D SPEND IT ON HOSPITALS, ROADS 'N' SCHOOLS
IF I HAD 800 MILLION DOLLARS
MY INFRASTRUCTURE PROGRAM WOULD BE COOL
IF I HAD 800 MILLION DOLLARS...
WE WOULDN'T HAVE TO EAT JIGG'S DINNER
(OF COURSE WE WOULD, WE'D JUST EAT MORE.)
BARENAKED DANNY— ALWAYS ON TOUR!

2009, The Telegram
WHO'S YOUR DANNY?
POPULAR REASON WHY MORE BABIES BORN IN '08...

HEY, PEOPLE—
DON'T BE SO
NEGATIVE!
OIL
OIL
OIL
OIL
OIL

DANNY, B'Y—ARE YOU NUTS? IF YOU PUT UP TRANSMISSION LINES HERE, MAYBE YOU SHOULD CALL THIS PLACE GROSS MORNE?!
2009-
KT.

HURRICANE DANNY
WASHROOM HAND DRYER FULL OF HOT AIR
2009
KT
The Telegram

ENERGIZER DANNY...
STOP HYDRO QUEBEC
...KEEPS GOIN'... AND GOIN'....
2009
KT.
The Telegram

DON'T WORRY ABOUT ANY OIL SPILL HERE. NOT UNDER MY WATCH!
OIL
OIL
DANNY KEEPS FOCUS ON OIL...
2010
KT
The Telegram

DA MULLET

DANNY SAYS:
"USE HOCKEY STICKS—
NOT HAKAPIKS!"
MAKE THE SEAL HUNT MORE HUMANE.
2006.
The Telegram

The Telegram.
KT
2003
WILLIAM'S
QUIET CONFIDENCE

KT. 2003
The Telegram
DANNY MILLIONS NEW ICEBERG ALLEY
BEER
I'M BRIDGIN' THE GAP TO LABRADOR AN' THE MAINLAND!

GET THE FEELIN' THAT SOMEBODY'S READY TO STRIKE?
STRIKE
2004
KT
the Telegram

I SEE DRUNK LEGISLATORS... WHAT DO YOU SEE?
2004.
KT

2004.
KT
The Telegram
I'M GOIN' TO CALL AN' SETTLE THIS STRIKE ISSUE ONCE AN' FOR ALL...
LOYOLA, ARE YOU CALLING LEO PUDDISTER?
NO, BILL ROWE!

IT'S A NO-BRAINER! PEOPLE HAVE A RIGHT TO KNOW WHAT'S GOING ON IN THE MINDS OF POLITICIANS!
WILLIAMS WANTS A MORE OPEN AND TRANSPARENT GOV-ERNMENT...
The Telegram
KT 2004.

KT. the Telegram
2004.
JEEPERS! I WISH PUDDISTER WOULD GET OFF MY BACK!

DANNY— IF YOU COULD WALK IN OUR SHOES... YOU'D PAY UP THE DUES...
DO THE RIGHT THING ON PAY EQUITY
2005.
PUDDISTER COMES OUT IN SUPPORT OF FEMALE NAPE WORKERS...

TO PROTECT THE RIGS FROM FALLING ROCKETS, ROCKET DAN SENDS IN HIS HIGHLY-TRAINED NAVY SEALS...
DON'T WORRY, B'YS... THE AMERICANS WILL NEVER DROP ANYTHING ON YOU GUYS!
2005.
KT
The Telegram

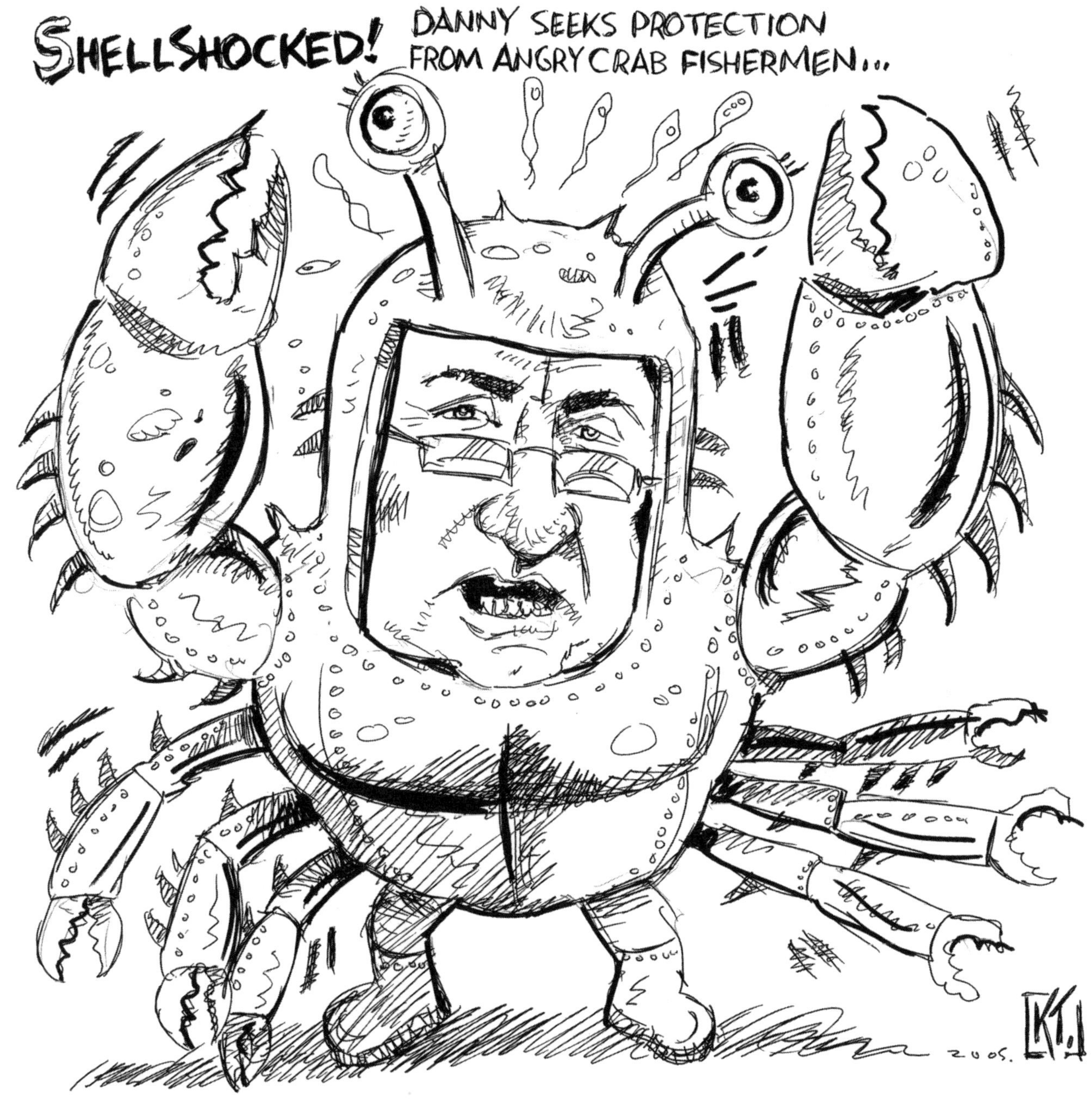
SHELLSHOCKED!
DANNY SEEKS PROTECTION FROM ANGRY CRAB FISHERMEN...
2005.
KT

DANNY'S ANTICS INSPIRE PLANS FOR PROPOSED FIXED LINK TO CANADA...
KT.
2005.

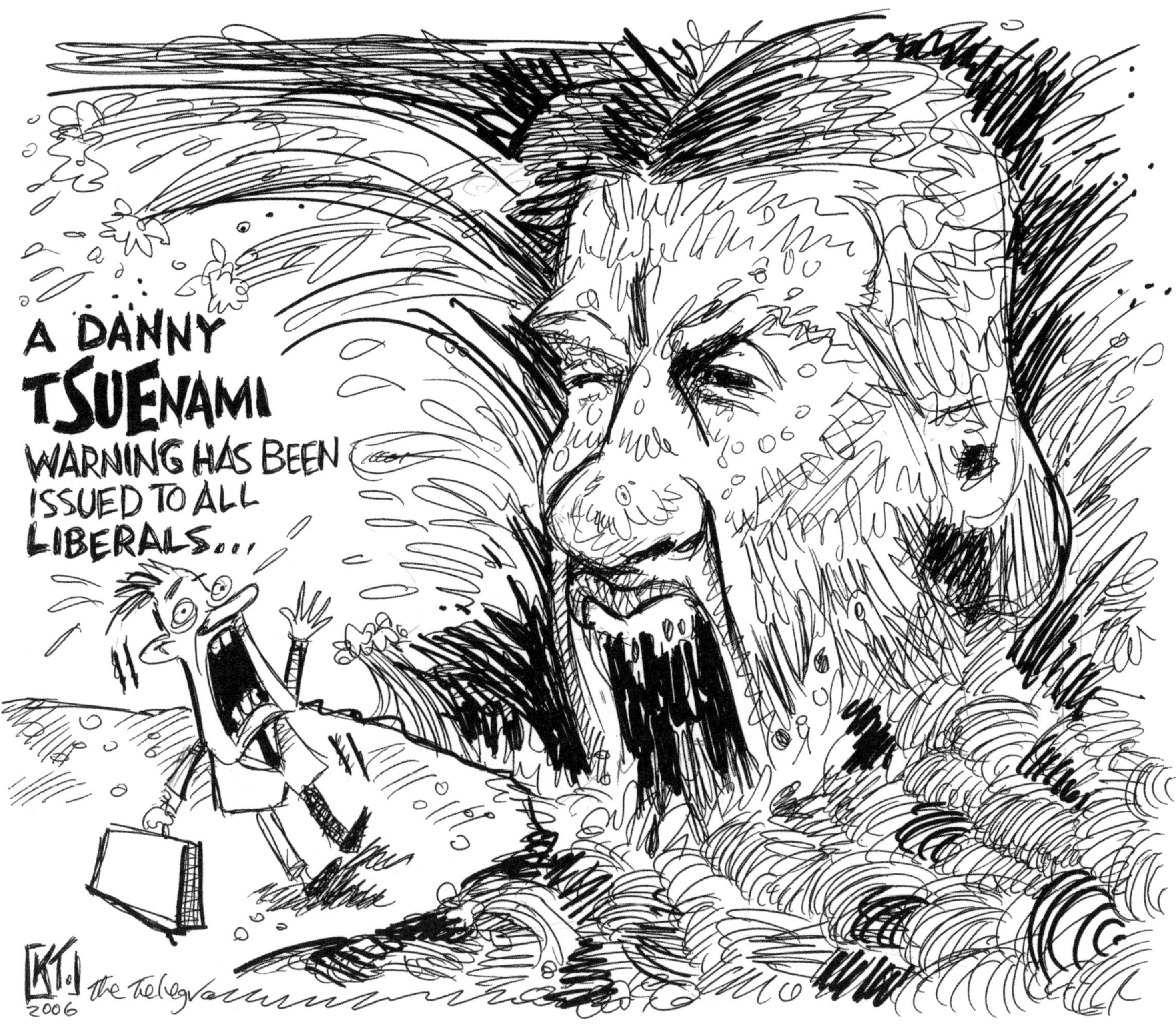
A DANNY TSUENAMI WARNING HAS BEEN ISSUED TO ALL LIBERALS...
KT
2006

The Telegram
2007.
SORRY, DAN,
I'M RETIRED!
-LOYOLA

GRRRRR....
TORY MHAS
DOUBLE BILLING
IS MAKING ME
SEE DOUBLE....
2007.

DEODORANT BODYSPRAY
DAN
DRIVES VOTERS WILD!
POPULAR AND SEXY...
ALL PC CANDIDATES CAN GO FROM SWEATY TO SWEETY WITH A QUICK SPRAY OF DAN! KILLS POLITICAL ODOR— AND MOST VOTERS LOVE THE POPULAR FRAGANCES.
WARNING:
PLEASE USE CONSERVATIVELY. NOT MEANT TO BE USED IN LIBERAL DOSES.
2007

WHAT WILL HAPPEN TO GERRY REID... FAME OR SHAME?

MY CAMPAIGN SLOGAN: "SAVE YOUR ENERGY: VOTE DANNY!"
DANNY'S ENERGY PLAN
2007
KT
The Telegram

DANNY HAS SAME PLATFORM ON COMBATTING CRIME OR FIGHTING NEXT MONTH'S ELECTION...
OLICE LINE DO NOT CROSS
DO NOT CROSS
2007

I'D LIKE TO CONGRATULATE DANNY WITH A HIGH FIVE... BUT I'M TOO BUSY. SO...
NOT BUSY
BUSY
BUSY
BUSY
BUSY
2007
KT.

PECKFORD'S COMMENTS ARE SO '80s! "BOO HOO, GAG ME WITH A SPRUNG..."
The Telegram
2007

THAT @☆#!? WHO TOLD POLICE
I WAS DRIVING AND USING MY
CELLPHONE! AARGH... WAIT—
I GOT AN IDEA...

* ONE OF THE BENEFITS OF BEING
A ROAD'S SCHOLAR...

DANNY'S EXCLUSIVE **HANDS FREE CELL...**

BLAH
BLAH
BLAH
BLAH

LOOKOUT, STEVE...
IT'S
DANBO
2008
[KT.]

2008.
KT
The Telegram
WATSON WAS EVERY INCH
A TERRORIST...
A VILE, DISGUSTIN' ANTI-SEALIN'
ACTIVIST...
HE'S BEEN LIVIN' LARGE
OFF THE SEAL HUNT PROTEST...
HE SHOULD BE BANNED UPON OUR
BRIGHT BLUE SEA...

I'M No.1...
I'M No.1!
STANLEY CUP
2008

KT
The Telegram
2008
MEMORIAL
UNIVERSITY
JOAN
BIG
DAN
ON
CAMPUS

ST. JOHN'S MAPLE LEAFS
C
The Telegram
KT 2009
DANNY, YVONNE, AND LORRAINE–
NEXT WEEK ON 'BATTLE OF THE BLADES!'

MR. SPEAKER — I PROPOSE WE INTRODUCE A BILL TO CHANGE THE NAME OF THE OPPOSITION TO THE STOPPOSITION PARTY...
YVONNE, STOP BEING SO NEGATIVE. STOP ASKING ME QUESTIONS.
KT 2009

NTV NEWS HAIR-RAISING EXCLUSIVE... FILES FROM THE 1960's
REVEAL DANNY IS NOT THE FIRST PREMIER TO SPORT NEW HAIR...
WINK
DANNY-'DO
JOE-'FRO
2010
KT

I LIKE BRUSH CUTTING...
BUT I'M ALSO A BIG
FAN OF MULLETS...
DANNY CONSIDERS ACTION
ON MOOSE-VEHICLE ACCIDENTS.
The Telegram
2016
KT.

2009.
KT.
HI HO, HI HO ... MORE TIME OFF WORK WE GO!
HOUSE CLOSES... AGAIN!

HIS OILINESS

THE FATHER...

THE SON...

THE HOLY COD OF CONFEDERATION!

The Telegram
KT.
2004.
WILLIAMS SENDING MARTIN
A MESSAGE BY LOWERING
THE FLAG...

THE EQUALIZATION FORMULA...
2006
KT
BROKEN PROMISES = BROKEN RECORD
the Telegram

THEY LOVE ME...
THEY LOVE ME NOT...
THEY LOVE ME...
HOW COULD THEY NOT?
ACCORDING TO THE POLLS...
The Telegram
KT.J 2009

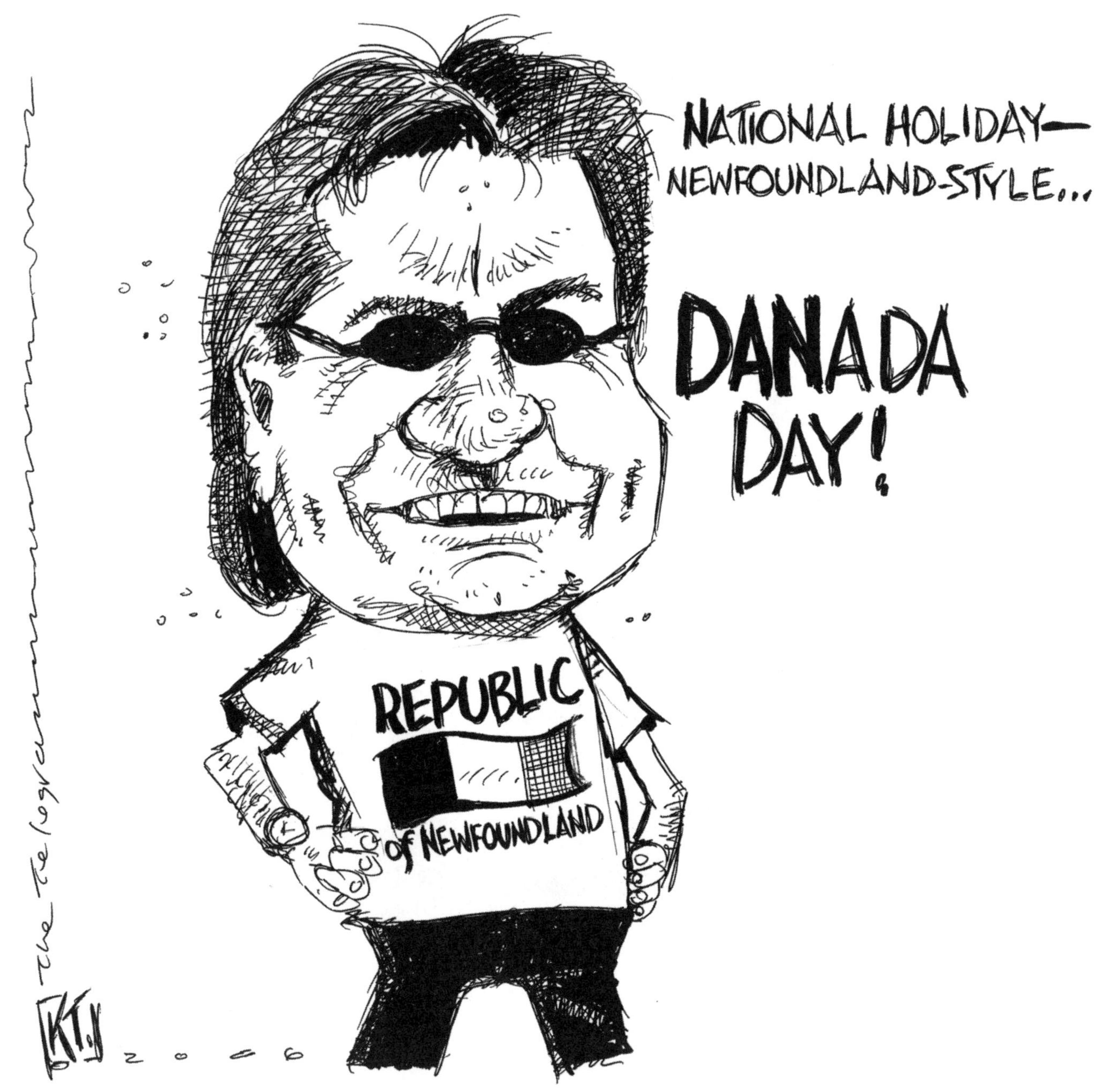
NATIONAL HOLIDAY—
NEWFOUNDLAND-STYLE...
DANADA DAY!
REPUBLIC
OF NEWFOUNDLAND

LUCY HARPER'S EQUALIZATION PROMISES...

GOOD GRIEF, DANNY... GO AHEAD. I WON'T PULL IT AWAY AGAIN... PROMISE!

The Telegram 2007.

PEOPLE WHO VOTE TORY IN THE NEXT ELECTION WILL GET A BIG RICH REWARD — ME!
The Telegram
2007. KT.

"OH, DANNY BOY—
ALBERTA, ALBERTA
IS CALL-ING...
FROM JOB TO JOB, WAY
DOWN CAL-GARY WAY.
MONEY'S GONE, AND
ALL MY EI IS DYING.
'TIS I, 'TIS I MUST GO
AND YOU, DAN, MUST STAY!
...BUT BRING ME BACK
WHEN HEBRON'S IN
PRO-DUCTION
OR WHEN ALL THE OIL AND JOBS
AND $$BILLIONS FLOW.
THEN I'LL BE HOME
IN SUNSHINE OR
IN FOG...
DANNY BOY, OH DANNY
BOY, WE LOVES
YOU SO!"
OUR ANTHEM 'ODE TO NEWFOUNDLAND' CHANGED TO 'OH, DANNY BOY'...
The Telegram
2007
KT

Gas
REGULAR
SUPREME
2007

DANNY "JAGGER"
ROCK GOD....
2007.

DESPITE WARNINGS, PRIME MINISTER HARPER DECIDES TO GO AHEAD AND MEET THE **DANI LAMA**!

DANNY ON HARPER
LIAR!
DANNY ON VOTES
BUY'ER!

2007

—NOW PLAYING—
THE DANTA CLAUSE 3
DANTA GIVES STEVE FROST THE COLD SHOULDER!
the Telegram
[KT.]
2007

DANNY AND HIS
IMAGINARY FRIEND
STEVELUPAGUS...
the Telegram
KT
2007

2008
KT
REMEMBER, DANNY—
NOTHIN' FLOWS FROM
OTTAWA TO NEWFOUND-
LAND UNLESS IT GOES
THROUGH ME, LOYOLA,
FIRST!
The Telegram

HEY, LOYOLA...HOW HARD IS IT TO FINALLY RETIRE FROM POLITICS...
...AS EASY AS A-B-C!
KT. The Telegram

ALL I SAID TO MEMORIAL'S PRESIDENT SEARCH COM-MITTEE WAS THAT THERE HAS TO BE ANOTHER SMART, QUALIFIED, RHODES SCHOLAR, LAWYER, BUSINESSMAN, MILLIONAIRE POLITICIAN OUT THERE SOMEWHERE IN THIS PROVINCE...
2008

2008.
—READER, COULD YOU TELL STEVE THAT HIS GREENHOUSE GAS KEPT ME AWAKE ALL NIGHT!
—READER, TELL DANNY HOW MUCH I HATE HIM GRINDING HIS TEETH IN HIS SLEEP!

STEVE 'N' I WANT TO GIVE 'ER ANOTHER SHOT...
MARRIAGE COUNSELOR
2008
KT.

HARPER'S NEW PROBLEMS GOT ME THINKIN' ABOUT CHANGIN' MY 'ABC' TO 'LOL'...
SNICKER
SNICKER
SNICKER
KT
2008

HAVE
THINK I'LL STILL HANG ON TO THIS FOR AWHILE...
NOT
The Telegram
2008.
KT.

THE ECONOMIC SLUMP CAUSES PROVINCE TO RECONSIDER BIG 'HAVE' CELEBRATIONS...
HAVE
PARTY BUS
THE 'HAVE' PARTY
...WE GOT THIS PARTY BUS RENTED AND PLAN TO TRAVEL ALL OVER THE PROVINCE (EXCEPT RURAL AREAS, GRAND FALLS-WINDSOR, LABRADOR, ETC.)
2009

I DON'T GET IT... DANNY WANTS ME TO SEND A VALENTINE TO STEVE...
BUT INSTEAD OF HITTING HARPER WITH AN ARROW, DANNY WANTS ME TO USE A HAKAPIK!
2009
K.
HAPPY VALENTINE'S

...TELL STEVE THAT I'M NOT QUITE READY YET TO RELEASE THE HOUNDS!
A B C
2009
KT
The Telegram

SEXY SENATOR MIKE DUFFY...
DANNY, I'M BIGGER THAN YOU AND HIGHER UP THE FOOD CHAIN...
2008

2009.
THE MOST INTERESTING DAN in the WORLD.
I DON'T ALWAYS DRINK RUM, BUT WHEN I DO.... I PREFER SCREECH!
NEWFOUNDLAND
SCREECH
Rum/Rhum
STAY THIRSTY, my friends.

POLLS SHOW DANNY STILL GETS OUR SEAL OF APPROVAL!
SMOOCH!
2009
K.
The Telegram

OF COURSE WE WON THE TERRA NOVA B'YELECTION... WHY? 'CUZ... I'SE DA B'Y!
The Telegram
KT
2009

2009
KT
LOOKING BACK ON THE DECADE, IN GENERAL, AND ON 2009, IN PARTICULAR, THE MOST POPULAR PERSON IN OUR PROVINCE AND COUNTRY — WAS ME! OBVIOUSLY, I'M THE BEST THING IN MOST PEOPLE'S BORING AND PATHETIC LIVES! MY ONLY WISH FOR YOU IS THAT 2010 BRINGS YOU MORE OF WHAT MAKES YOU FEEL WARM AND FUZZY INSIDE — ME! SO... PLEASE JOIN ALL OF ME IN WISHING ALL OF YOU A HAPPY ME YEAR!
DAN of the DECADE
The Telegram

STEVE,
EDITOR'S NOTE: DUE TO THIS BEING A FAMILY NEWSPAPER, WE CANNOT PRINT THE ABOVE CAPTION. PLEASE FEEL FREE TO INSERT YOUR OWN COMMENTS, IF YOU WISH. THANK YOU.
2009
KT
The Telegram

DICTATOR DAN

LIBYAN LEADER MAY VISIT PROVINCE FOR ANNUAL
DICTATORS ANONYMOUS CONVENTION
GADHAFI, WHO DOES YOUR MULLET?
2009

MARSHALL SPEAKS OUT...

CABINET MINISTERS LEFT SPEECHLESS AS WILLIAMS UN-VEILS NEW UNIFORM FOR GOVERNMENT MEMBERS...
KINGDOM OF DICTATOR DAN
2004
KT

DANNY'S VALENTINE
FOR CIVIL SERVANTS...
KISS ME!
2004
KT
the Telegram.

DAN
THE DRACONIAN!
NAPE
CUPE
2004.

CONFEDERATION BUILDING WELCOMING COMMITTEE...

KT. 2005.

The Telegram

RNC

RIOT

THIS WAY!

CLONES OR WHA...?

DAN

DARTH

The Telegram

WE MEAN BUSINESS...
YOU MEAN... OUTTA BUSINESS!
2005.
KT.
VOCM
NTV
Stephenville
GRAND FALLS-WINDSOR

DIDN'T DANNY PROMISE THE MILL WOULDN'T CLOSE ON HIS WATCH...?
ZZZZZZZ
DAN'S Security
STEPHENVILLE
SECURITY
2006.
KT.
The Telegram

DANNY SUPPORTS WOMEN'S MOVEMENT...
THERE'S THE DOOR, LADIES...
The Telegram
2005
KT

LISTEN TO MY VOICE ONLY, TREVOR! 'IF YOU WANT TO ACT LIKE A BIGWIG— YOU NEED TO THINK LIKE A BIGWIG.' RIGHT, B'YS?
Y-YES M-MASTER...
2005
KT.
the Telegram

"NOW, MY DEAR FELLOW NEWFOUNDLANDERS... WE SHOULD NOT BE TOO CRITICAL... SHOULD NOT SHOUT... SHOULD NOT WHINE! WE SHOULD BE GRATEFUL WE HAVE ALL THESE MARVELOUS HOSPITAL BUILDINGS AND DOCTORS TO CARE FOR US! WE DO NOT WANT DISCORD IN THIS GREAT DECENT CHRISTIAN PROVINCE..."
The Telegram
2008.
KT

GOVERNMENT HOPES BABY BUCKS INCENTIVE SPURS NEW YOUTH FORCE— THE YOUNG WILLIAMS!
2008
KT

AND NOW... A FEW WORDS FROM DANNY'S RIGHT HAND MAN— JEROME...
MR. SPEAKER, THE INQUIRY WILL BE TOO LONG AND TOO EXPENSIVE!, THE LAWYERS ARE TOO PROSECUTORIAL!, SQUAWK DANNY IS GREAT!
The Telegram
2008
KT

...AS THE DAN OF THE HOUSE, YVONNE, I'M SAYING THE HONEYMOON IS OVER! I MAKE THE RULES – LIKE IT OR LUMP IT! AND... NO MORE MONEY! NOW – BRING ME MY SLIPPERS...
The Telegram
2008

2008
KT.
THE BUCK STOPS HERE
...UNLESS, OF COURSE, IT GOT LOST SOMEWHERE ALONG THE WAY AT EASTERN HEALTH OR IN THE MEDIA!
The Telegram

SOMETIMES...
IT'S APPROPRIATE
TO EXPROPRIATE!
2008.
ABITIBIBOWATER
MILL
DAN BUNYAN

(SNIFF)...
...AND THEN TO GET UDANIMOUS SUPPORT IN THE HOUSE OF ASSEMBLY...(SNIFF, SNIFF) I HAVEN'T SEEN SO MANY SMILING MHAs SINCE WE HANDED OUT BIG CONSTITUENCY ALLOWANCES!
2008
KT
The Telegram

DANNY'S NEW FLAG...

KT.

The Telegram

2009

2009.
The Telegram
DANNY, DON'T SHOOT THE MESSENGER...
...'CUZ ME NERVES ARE ALREADY SHOT!
POPULAR LAB COATS AT EASTERN HEALTH...

@☆!!#
ARE YOU KIDDING?
AN APOLOGY TO
EASTERN HEALTH??
I SHOULD REALLY BE
APOLOGIZING FOR
PUTTING WISEMAN IN
AS HEALTH MINISTER!
2009
The Telegram

SIMMS...I DON'T HAVE TO LISTEN TO THIS CRAP! WITH MY MONEY, I'LL BUY VOCM AND RENAME IT "VOCD"—VOICE OF THE COMMON DAN!
#@!
VOCM
BLADES
2009
The Telegram

2009
KT.
I THINK IT'S QUITE OBVIOUS WHERE I STAND...
The Telegram
BACK BENCHER VERGE STANDS UP FOR DISTRICT

I SUPPORT FREEDOM OF INFORMATION. GO AHEAD— ASK...
...I ALSO SUPPORT MY FREEDOM TO NOT LISTEN— LALALALALALA I CAN'T HEAR YOU!
2009.

ONLY YOU TRULY UNDERSTAND ME, MINI DANNY ME!.
The Telegram
2009
KT

TROUBLE IS HIS BUSINESS. AND BUSINESS IS GOOD.
2010
REPUBLIC OF DANNY
SERIES PREMIER.

2010 the Telegram
YEAH? WELL...
#@@★OFF!
RING
RING
RING RING
RING RING
RING RING
RING
COMPLAINTS
DEPT.

MY HEART...
MY HEALTH...
MY BAD!
DW
2010
KT
The Telegram
RECOVERING UNDER THE FLORIDA SUN...

HEY, DOC—YOUR CONTRACT DEMANDS ARE THROUGH THE ROOF!
KT.
2010

DON'T BELIEVE
THEM DOCTORS...
I'LL TELL THE TRUTH,
THE WHOLE TRUTH AND
NOTHING BUT THE TRUTH...
SO HELP ME DAN!
2010

ON EASTERN HEALTH...
THEY SHOULD BE SHOT...
ON H1N1 VACCINE...
THEY SHOULD GET A SHOT...
The Telegram
2009
K.

ACKNOWLEDGEMENTS

Front cover: Design, Derek Mills; illustration, Kevin Tobin.
Back cover: Thanks to my daughter Jessica for her wonderful painting.

Special thanks to Senator Fabian Manning for the Foreword.

And thank you, Donna Francis and Creative Publishers, for all your assistance and support.

BIOGRAPHY

Kevin Tobin's (KT.) editorial cartoons have been a regular feature of *The Telegram*'s editorial page for over 20 years. KT. has published ten books on his cartoons and has received a Silver Award of Excellence at the Atlantic Journalism Awards. His colourful caricatures can be found on the walls of offices and rec rooms throughout our province.

Kevin first began his doodling in diapers...his teenage years saw him drawing on his comic book heroes for inspiration. Later, politicians like Crosbie, Mulroney, Wells, Chretien, Tobin & company fueled his fire for creativity and commentary. These days, KT. is keeping a close eye on the ongoing shenanigans of Danny and that crowd in the Confederation Building.

While cartooning and family are his passion, he also loves his day job at m5, and greatly appreciates running, friends, hockey, coaching, and barbecuing.